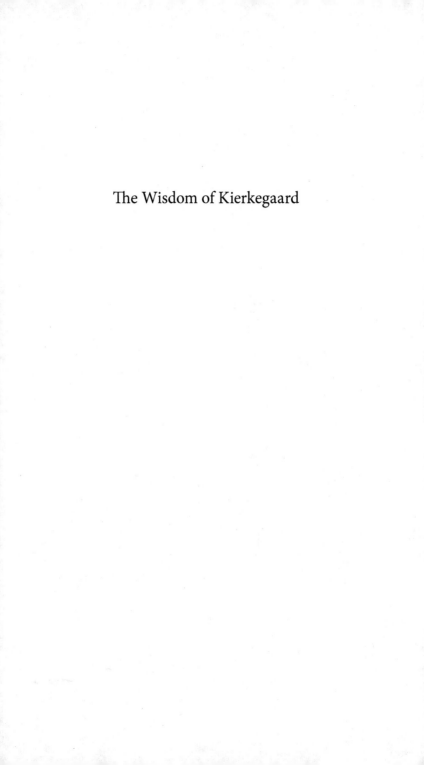

The Wisdom of Kierkegaard

The Wisdom of Kierkegaard

A Collection of Quotations on Faith and Life

$\approx$

Clifford Williams

WIPF *&* STOCK · Eugene, Oregon

THE WISDOM OF KIERKEGAARD
A Collection of Quotations on Faith and Life

Wipf & Stock
A Division of Wipf and Stock Publishers
199 W. 8th Ave., Suite 3
Eugene, OR 97401

www.wipfandstock.com

ISBN 13: 978-1-60608-485-4

Manufactured in the U.S.A.

CONTENTS

ABBREVIATIONS

Citations in the text use the following abbreviations:

CD	*Christian Discourses*
CUP	*Concluding Unscientific Postscript*
D	*The Diary of Soren Kierkegaard*
EO	*Either/Or*
EUD	*Eighteen Upbuilding Discourses*
FSE	*For Self-Examination*
FT	*Fear and Trembling*
JFY	*Judge for Yourself!*
JP	*Søren Kierkegaard's Journals and Papers*
PC	*Practice in Christianity*
SLW	*Stages on Life's Way*
SUD	*The Sickness unto Death*
TDIO	*Three Discourses on Imagined Occasions*
UDVS	*Upbuilding Discourses in Various Spirits*
WA	*Without Authority*
WL	*Works of Love*

INTRODUCTION

Tucked away in the complicated prose that fills many of Søren Kierkegaard's books are numerous insightful declarations. They arrest the reader with their depth of understanding. They often are expressed in a lilting and lyrical manner. Encountering them makes working through the intricate prose eminently worthwhile.

This book contains 250 such passages. I have chosen them partly because they can be understood apart from their context and partly because they prompt the reader to think, "Ah! That's true." Many of them contain a twist that gives an incisive jab. Some are on themes for which Kierkegaard is well-known, but many are on a variety of other significant themes.

Søren Kierkegaard lived in Denmark from 1813 to 1855. The Danish church at that time was an official extension of the government. The pastors' salaries were paid by the government, and citizens who wished to form alternative congregations were frowned upon. Kierkegaard thought that the Danish church had departed from the New Testament ideal. He thought, in fact, that the Danish church did not exemplify Christianity at all. So he made it his life's aim to reintroduce Christianity into the church. This could not be done simply by restating the truths of Christianity, however, for those in the church regarded themselves as believers. They would have been offended at the implication, or direct charge, that they did not really believe. Reintroducing Christianity could be done, Kierkegaard thought, only indirectly. This meant that he would have to produce a psychological analysis of the causes of unbelief and describe extensively what genuine faith should be.

For Kierkegaard, the most important cause of unbelief, at least in Denmark, was individuals' thoughtless identification with the church. His favorite term for the church was "the crowd." What happens, he thought, is that individuals so identify with the crowd that they lose their own identity. In a sense they become one with the crowd. This means that what they think of as being their faith is not really theirs. It is the crowd's faith.

Although Kierkegaard's concern was for those in the Danish church, he has pinpointed a phenomenon that is universal. We humans find it alluring to identify with some group. In this identification we find security. The group is established and stable, so identifying with it gives us the sense of being established and stable. It is a fearful thing to stand alone. We would have nothing to back us up if we did, nothing to validate us. And we desperately need validation.

What Kierkegaard saw, then, is that in a religious context, we use this identification as a substitute for real faith. The identification is, in fact, a way of hiding from God. It is a way of evading the responsibility we need to take for our faith. And it is the most ruinous evasion possible, he asserted, partly because we do not know we have done it, and partly because it makes us think we have real faith when in fact we do not.

Faith, then, for Kierkegaard is something we must have for ourselves. To paraphrase one of his statements in "Faith" (p. 32), a group can do much for its members—it can give them security and a sense of belonging—but it cannot give them faith. Ultimately, we stand alone before God. And ultimately it is only we who can have faith.

Faith has a number of other features as well. Its inner core is earnestness. It exhibits searching restlessness. It springs from a longing for God. It rests on God's grace. It requires being honest with oneself. It excises self-satisfaction. It results in adopting the right priorities.

Kierkegaard's analysis of unbelief and his concern with the nature of faith form the context of the following passages. Some of the passages bear directly on these themes and some bear indirectly. All of the passages deal with what Kierkegaard designates the "call from eternity." This call comes both early and late, and, as these passages amply demonstrate, it involves a wide variety of attitudes, desires, and motives.

I have given the passages titles and have alphabetized them. In addition, I have introduced each alphabetical section with a page of thoughts on one of the themes in the section. It is my hope, as it is Kierkegaard's, that readers will be moved by his reflections to meditate deeply on what matters most in life.

A

We become anxious when we imagine what it would be like to be alone, Kierkegaard says—alone not just for a time and not just with respect to our friends and acquaintances, but overlooked by everyone and forgotten by God. In this aloneness, no one would notice us as we walked along a busy city sidewalk. We would get no mail and no telephone calls. Our parents would forget us. None of our letters would be answered. No one would respond to our pleas to be listened to or take any initiative to communicate with us. Terror would not be too strong a reaction to this kind of aloneness.

Kierkegaard also observes that we thwart this terror by connecting ourselves with others. We form close friendships with one or two people, less close friendships with eight or ten, and acquire acquaintances by the dozen. Doing so is good, no doubt, but, Kierkegaard declared, it is not enough to keep cosmic anxiety at bay. Our friends and acquaintances die, and in the end they cannot rescue us. The terror comes back.

The remedy for terror is to connect ourselves to God, one who is not finite and who will not die. But, declares Kierkegaard, this we are reluctant to do. We are afraid to approach God by ourselves. We shrink from taking full responsibility for our destiny. So we look to others to corroborate our connection. We imitate what we think is their connection. We lose ourselves in them, that is, identify with them, because we think that by doing so we will acquire the attachment to God that they have or think they have. Doing this, of course, does not get us attached to God. For that, we need "primitivity"—being alone with God without the mediation of other people.

So we are caught in a dilemma. We desire desperately to avoid cosmic aloneness. The way we are most inclined to avoid this aloneness—connecting ourselves with others—will not work. And we are afraid of adopting the only remedy that will work.

What can we do?

This question is one an evangelist might pose—not a front-door evangelist, one who barrels in with direct and straightforward declarations—but a backdoor evangelist, one who slips in with questions and dilemmas, oblique observations, and roundabout insights. The aim of the backdoor evangelist is to provoke those who regard themselves as having faith to think acutely about whether their faith is real.

One way of reading Kierkegaard is to regard him as a backdoor evangelist. He wants to prod people to become faith possessors. His insights are aimed not just at understanding faith but at arousing it.

～

ACCEPTING COMFORT

While the worried one sadly suffers with another, his mind is set at ease. The person who armed himself against comfort is now disarmed; the person who was like a fortified city is now like a city that has surrendered; by grieving with someone else, he himself finds comfort. (*UDVS,* 202)

ADMIRATION AND ENVY

If I take it into my head that I would very much like to resemble or be that which is admired, something else may easily happen, namely, that my admiration changes to envy. (*PC,* 241)

ALIENATION

A person cannot be as alienated by the indifference to his faith on the part of those who have another faith, another God, as he must feel alienated by the indifference of those who say they have the same faith. (*CD,* 243)

ALONE

Deep within every human being there still lives the anxiety over the possibility of being alone in the world, forgotten by God, overlooked among the millions and millions in this enormous household. One keeps this anxiety at a distance by looking at the many round about who are related to him as kin and friends, but the anxiety is still there, nevertheless, and one hardly dares think of how he would feel if all this were taken away. (*JP,* I, 40)

ALONE WITH GOD

For primitivity—having to be primitive, alone with God without being preceded by others whom one can ape and to whom one can refer for corroboration—is something people accept most reluctantly. (*D*, 162)

ANXIETY

Anxiety is a desire for what one fears, a sympathetic antipathy; anxiety is an alien power which grips the individual, and yet one cannot tear himself free from it and does not want to, for one fears, but what he fears he desires. Anxiety makes the individual powerless. (*JP*, I, 39)

Time goes slowly for the anxious, and for the very anxious even one moment is deadly slow, and for someone anxious unto death time finally stands still. (*EUD*, 345)

APPEARANCES

People are willing enough to practice compassion and self-denial, willing enough to seek after wisdom, etc., but they want to determine the criterion themselves, that it shall be to *a certain degree*. They do not wish to do away with all these glorious virtues; on the contrary, they want—at a cheap price—to have as comfortably as possible the appearance of and the reputation for practicing them. (*PC*, 60)

"AT LAST . . ."

There is a little phrase that is familiar enough to congregations, even though not always heeded by them. Little and insignificant as it seems, it nevertheless is pregnant with meaning; it is quiet and yet so stirring, calm and yet so full of longing. It is the phrase "at last," for in this way end many of the sacred collects that are read in the churches: "and then at last obtain eternal salvation." The older person among us, who is almost within reach of the goal, gazes back in thought over the road he has traveled. He recollects the course of events, and the faded figures become vivid again. He is overwhelmed by the abundant content of his experience; he is weary and says: and then at last obtain eternal salvation. The younger person, who still stands at the beginning of the road, gazes in thought out over the long course, experiences in thought what is to come: the painful privations, the secret troubles, the sad longings, the fearful spiritual trials. He is weary of mind and says: and then at last obtain eternal salvation. Yes, it would indeed be a great gift if a person could rightly use this phrase; yet no person learns this from another, but each one individually learns it only from and through God. (*EUD,* 28)

AVOIDANCE

On the whole, it is incredible how cunning and inventive people are in avoiding the final decision. (*CUP,* I, 423)

B

Kierkegaard spent a good deal of time trying to show how hard it is to be a Christian. Most Christian writers, he observed, try to make it easier to be a believer, but he adopted it as his aim to show how strenuous it is.

It is a matter of honesty, Kierkegaard would say. If we want to become believers, we can not delude ourselves into thinking that doing so is easy. If we want to make our way to eternity, we will not be able to get there by sauntering along. If we desire to love well, we will not be able to do so without working at it for a lifetime. To think that being a Christian is easy, accordingly, causes one not to be one, which, for Kierkegaard, would be a deadly tragedy.

If we thought for a few minutes about the hard features of the Christian life, we could easily think of some. Here are several that might occur to us.

1. Acquiring new habits. We want to hang on to our old, dearly beloved habits. We resist exchanging them for new habits we know we should adopt.

2. Asking for forgiveness. We want to believe that we are in the right, that we always desire what is good, and that we are decent persons who are worthy of admiration.

3. Staying in love with one person our whole life, even if that person has deeply hurt us. Our first response is to flee from one who has wounded us.

4. Acknowledging that we will die. We deny our own deaths. We find it nearly impossible to believe that what we are familiar with and care about will come to an end.

5. Maintaining a lively inner energy. We lose energy and want simply to let life slide by.

Demonstrating how hard each of these is may not be what readers want, but it would be truthful. And describing how hard these are may prompt some readers to rise to the challenge.

∾

BATTLING

The soul must fight many a hard battle and many a time must begin from the beginning. (*EUD*, 200)

BECOMING A CHRISTIAN

Not until a man has become so utterly unhappy, or has grasped the woefulness of life so deeply that he is moved to say, and mean it: life for me has no value—not till then is he able to make a bid for Christianity. (*D*, 150)

It is the same with Christianity or with becoming a Christian as it is with all radical cures. One postpones it as long as possible. (*JP*, I, 168)

BEING A CHILD

One can be thirty years old and more, forty years old, and still be just a child—yes, one can die as an aged child. (*EUD*, 316)

BEING SOMETHING

The purely human view thinks that becoming something is the way to become sober. Christianity thinks that becoming nothing—before God—that precisely this is the way, and that wanting to be something before God, if anyone could hit upon such an idea, is intoxication. (*JFY*, 106)

BELIEVING

Christ himself understood as no human being can understand how difficult it is to become a believer. (*PC*, 99)

THE BIRTH PAINS OF LOVE

Must wisdom be bought, understanding be bought, peace of mind be bought, the blessedness of heaven be bought, must life be bought in the pain of birth, but love is not supposed to know any birth pains? (*EUD*, 73)

BOREDOM

The person who is without God in the world soon becomes bored with himself—and expresses this haughtily by being bored with all life, but the person who is in fellowship with God indeed lives with the one whose presence gives infinite significance to even the most insignificant. (*TDIO*, 78)

BROODING ON SIN

That a person wants to sit and brood and stare at his sin and is unwilling to have faith that it is forgiven: is this also guilt in that it is a minimizing of what Christ has done. (*JP*, IV, 116)

BUILDING UP

Wherever upbuilding is, there is love, and wherever love is, there is upbuilding. (*WL*, 214)

BUSYNESS

Busyness makes it almost impossible for an individual to form a heart; on the other hand, the thinker, the poet, the religious person who has actually formed his heart never becomes popular, not because he is difficult, but because a quiet and protracted occupation and intimacy with oneself and a remoteness go along with it. (*JP*, II, 397)

This busyness is indeed like a spell. And how sad to note how its power grows with the increasing buzzing, how the spell spreads, seeks to trap the earlier prey so that childhood or youth are scarcely granted the stillness, the remoteness, in which the eternal attains a divine growth. (*UDVS*, 66)

In busyness there *is neither the time nor the tranquillity to acquire the transparency* that is necessary for understanding oneself in willing one thing or for just temporarily understanding oneself in one's unclarity. No, busyness—in which one continually goes further and further, and noise, in which the true is continually forgotten more and more, and the multitude of circumstances, incentives, and hindrances—continually makes it more impossible for one to gain any deeper knowledge of oneself. (*UDVS*, 67)

C

We humans are well practiced in self-deception. Although we genuinely desire to do what is good, we also want to evade it. But we do not want to know that we evade it. So we cleverly hide our evasions.

We may have heard that an acquaintance is in trouble, depressed, or hurt in some way. We become concerned, but we also become curious. What is going on with her? Who has hurt her? Is she so depressed that she is suicidal? Our cleverness substitutes curiosity for concern and makes us think that in satisfying our curiosity we are gaining knowledge that will increase our concern. We may indeed increase our concern by gaining knowledge, but in this case our motive is simply to satisfy curiosity, and cleverness hides that from us.

We may find ourselves wanting more from doing what is good than the intrinsic reward of doing it. So we look for further satisfaction—a look of admiration that an onlooker gives or a compliment from someone who hears about what we have done. We cleverly conceal the fact that we are using these further satisfactions as a substitute for the intrinsic reward. To use Kierkegaard's words, we earn a little on the side and thereby sidestep the good itself.

Of course, if we can describe the ways in which we cleverly deceive ourselves in these ways, as Kierkegaard does so extensively, we might suppose that we can just as cleverly uncover them. And indeed we can uncover them. But not always simply. And certainly not automatically. For we can think we have uncovered our evasions even though we have not. We may read insightful descriptions of evasions and recognize the truth in them, but still be evading. We can, that is, consciously distinguish genuine concern for someone's trouble from simple curiosity about those troubles, want to have only genuine concern, but still indulge ourselves in curiosity. This dividedness is one of the most fascinating, though disheartening, features of the human psyche. How, then, can we be sure that we are not at any given moment still evading?

Kierkegaard never decisively answers this question. His copious descriptions of evasions make one wonder whether we can be sure. Perhaps the most that can be said is that if we are to rid ourselves of evasions, it will have to be done slowly, with constant attention, and with more honesty than we are accustomed to. This may be the most acute lesson we can learn from reading Kierkegaard.

≈

CARES

Anyone who has cares, especially the more deeply and the longer they penetrate into the soul or the longer they penetrate it deeply, is perhaps also tempted to be impatiently unwilling to hear any human words about comfort and hope. (*UDVS*, 160)

CHEATING AT LIFE

There are many people who arrive at conclusions in life much the way schoolboys do; they cheat their teachers by copying the answer out of the arithmetic book without having worked the problem themselves. (*JP,* IV, 275)

CHEATING GOD

When a person has succeeded in killing the thought of God and every feeling and mood that like his emissaries bring him to mind, then that person lives on as if he were his own master, himself the architect of his fortune, himself the one who must take care of everything but also the one who is entitled to everything—that is, he cheats God of what is due him. (*CD,* 66-67)

CLEVERNESS

The decision is to will to do everything for the good—it is not sagaciously to will to have advantage from the good. Alas, but in every human being there is a power, a dangerous and also a great power. This power is *sagacity*. Sagacity is continually averse to the decision; it fights for its life and honor, because if the decision wins, then sagacity is the same as having been put to death, reduced to being a disdained servant, to whose words one pays great attention but whose advice one disdains to follow. (*UDVS,* 82)

The sagacious person's secret is that he cannot be totally satisfied with the good's meager reward but must earn a little on the side—by going around a little on the side. (*UDVS,* 87)

CLINGING TO SIN

There is nothing to which a human being so desperately firmly clings as to his sin. (*WA*, 143)

COMPARISON

A collected mind . . . has collected itself from all distraction and thus also from all comparison, whether it tempts to earthly and incidental despondency because the person comparing must himself confess that he is behind many others, or whether it tempts to arrogance because he, humanly speaking, seems to be further ahead than many others. (*UDVS*, 152)

COMPASSION

To make oneself quite *literally one with the most wretched* (and this, this alone is *divine* compassion), this is "too much" for people, something they can shed a few emotional tears over during a quiet Sunday hour. . . . The point is that it is too lofty for them to bear seeing it in daily use; it must be at a distance for them to be able to bear it. (*PC*, 59)

CONQUERING HARDSHIP

It is one thing to conquer in the hardship, to overcome the hardship as one overcomes an enemy, while continuing in the idea that the hardship is one's enemy; but it is more than conquering to believe that the hardship is one's friend, that it is not the opposition but the road, is not what obstructs but develops, is not what disheartens but ennobles. (*UDVS*, 303)

CONSUMED

The religious person has lost the relativity of immediacy, its diversion, its whiling away of time—precisely its whiling away of time. The absolute conception of God consumes him like the fire of the summer sun when it refuses to set, like the fire of the summer sun when it refuses to cease. (*CUP,* I, 485)

CONVENIENCE

What we want in fact is the most convenient religion possible, a kind of accompaniment to all our finite striving. (*JP,* III, 108)

CONVERSION

Conversion goes slowly. . . . It is easy to become impatient: if it cannot happen at once, one may just as well let it go, begin tomorrow, and enjoy today; this is the temptation. (*JP,* I, 171).

COWARDLINESS

Cowardliness prevents a person from *doing the good*, from accomplishing the truly great and noble to which he has attached himself in a resolution. (*EUD,* 363)

CROWD BEHAVIOR

One must see it for himself (otherwise he would not believe it), how even nice, good-natured people become like different creatures as soon as they form a "crowd." . . . The hardheartedness with which otherwise kind people act in the capacity of the public, because they regard their participation or nonparticipation as a small matter—a small matter which becomes enormous through the contribution of the many. (*JP*, III, 313)

CROWD FAITH

When Christ says (Matthew 10:17), "Beware of people," I wonder if by this is not also meant: Beware of being tricked out of the highest by people, that is, by continual comparison with other people, by habit, and by externals? The shadiness of a deceiver is not so dangerous—in fact, one becomes more readily aware of it; but this, to have the highest in a kind of indifferent fellowship, in the indolence of a habit, indeed, in the indolence of a habit that even wants to set the generation in place of the single individuals, wants to make the generation the recipient and the single individuals automatically sharers by virtue of that—this is a terrible thing. (*WL*, 27)

CULTURED CHRISTIANS

As understanding and culture and education increase, it becomes more and more difficult to sustain the passion of faith. . . . Thus cultured people have only a very ironic advantage over simple folk with regard to becoming and continuing to be Christians: the advantage that it is more difficult. (*CUP*, I, 606)

CUNNING RESISTANCE

A lack of conscience does not manifest itself as criminal acts—which would be foolish, stupid, and ill-advised—no, no, it manifests itself with moderation, to a certain degree, and then with taste and culture; it makes life cozy and enjoyable. (*FSE*, 40)

D

Spiritual danger is just as real as physical danger, but often we do not see it as clearly. The reason for this is that we do not want to be aware of it, or do not want to know about the severity of its threats. The trouble, of course, with being unaware of danger is that we cannot take precautions against it. We are more liable to succumb to it.

Kierkegaard points out a number of spiritual dangers. He says, for example, that "it is a common human craving to be looked upon as someone great." The danger here is that in succumbing to the craving, we will ignore or forget the poor, the oppressed, the disabled. We are uncomfortable thinking about these kinds of people, so we put the fact that we have the craving to be great out of mind, and thereby the danger that results from it.

Other unsettling facts receive the same treatment. In the grave we are all equal, Kierkegaard declared. The danger in not being attentive to this fact is that we will regard ourselves as worthy of distinction and honor. But we do not like to think about this danger, so we make ourselves "forget" the unsettling fact.

The true dangers of life are not our susceptibility to crime and road collisions, but our susceptibility to despair, our tendency to delay contrition, and the possibility of not dying well.

∾

DANGER

From the religious point of view, the greatest danger is that one does not discover, that one is not always discovering, that one is in danger. (*SLW,* 468)

DANISH CHRISTENDOM

To be a Christian has become a nothing, a silly game, something that everyone is as a matter of course, something one slips into more easily than one slips into the most trifling accomplishment. (*PC,* 67)

DEATH

Christianly understood, however, death is by no means the last of all; in fact, it is only a minor event within that which is all, an eternal life, and, Christianly understood, there is infinitely much more hope in death than there is in life. (*SUD,* 7–8)

In the grave every human being needs equally little. (*EUD,* 299)

That death can make a finish is indeed certain, but the challenge of earnestness to the living is to think it, to think that all is over, that there comes a time when all is over. This is the difficult thing, because even in the moment of death the dying person thinks that he still might have some time to live, and one is even afraid to tell him that all is over. (*TDIO*, 79)

DELAYED PENITENCE

If you have ever broken God's commandments, you certainly did not dare at the time to think about God, not even penitently. But after an interval of time in which you again did not sin, you gained the courage; it was as if your guilt had diminished somewhat because it was some time ago and during that time you had not sinned very often. (*JP*, IV, 467)

DESIRE FOR GREATNESS

It is a common human craving to be looked upon as someone great; and the common fakery is to pass oneself off for something more than one is. (*FSE*, 59)

DESPAIR

The common view that despair is a rarity is entirely wrong; on the contrary, it is universal. The common view, which assumes that everyone who does not think or feel he is in despair is not or that only he who says he is in despair is, is totally false. (*SUD*, 26)

DIFFICULTY

The person who chooses Christianity should at that very moment have an impression of its difficulty so that he can know what it is that he is choosing. A young person should not be promised anything other than what Christianity can keep, but Christianity cannot keep anything other than what it has promised from the beginning: the world's ingratitude, opposition, and derision, and continually to a higher degree the more earnest a Christian one becomes. (*WL*, 194)

DISHONESTY

Often there is lament over the great amount of dishonesty in trade and business, etc.

Ah, the tragedy is that in no relationship is there so much dishonesty as in the most important one, which concerns the soul's salvation, eternal happiness, Christianity—that here even the most honest person of all is somewhat dishonest. And why is he like this; what is the source of this? It comes from the fact that every man is afraid of eternity, of its enormous power, afraid of getting involved in earnest with it. And just because we human beings are all afraid, we share a kind of mutual human honesty—we all stick together in being dishonest. (*JP*, I, 386)

DISTINCTIONS EVEN IN DEATH

If you go out there earlier in the morning, when the sun peeps vivaciously through the branches, you will find everything so nicely decorated. The small families each have their own little plot for themselves, approximately the same size. . . . Yet there is a minor distinction, like a droll reminder of the distinction which was so enormous in the world; if there is a distinction here, it is a matter of inches for one to have more than the other. Having a flower on one's grave already amounts to a big difference, and having a tree is prosperity—alas, thus life returns in death, for in childhood owning a flower was already a big thing, and to own a tree extraordinary.

Even in the middle of an earnest contemplation of death, one has to smile—not at the equality of all, but that there still continue to be distinctions. (*JP*, I, 336)

DOING

The real simplicity, the truly simple exposition of the essentially Christian is—to do it.

But to do it—that is an effort, an effort like the struggle of death, inasmuch as it means to die to; but to give an exposition of Christianity—that is a pleasure. (*JFY*, 116)

DOMINEERING PERSON

The rigid, the domineering person lacks flexibility, lacks the pliability to comprehend others; he demands his own from everyone, wants everyone to be transformed in his image, to be trimmed according to his pattern for human beings. (*WL*, 270)

DOUBT

Doubt is a deep and crafty passion, but he whose soul is not gripped by it so inwardly that he becomes speechless is only shamming this passion. (*EUD*, 23)

Doubt is sly and guileful, not at all loudmouthed and defiant, as it is sometimes proclaimed to be; it is unassuming and crafty, not brash and presumptuous, and the more unassuming it is, the more dangerous it is. (*EUD*, 41)

DYING TO SELF

The first thing the life-giving Spirit says is that you must enter into death. . . . You must first die to every merely earthly hope, to every merely human confidence; you must die to your selfishness. (*FSE*, 76–77)

DYING WELL

To die is indeed the lot of every human being and thus is a very mediocre art, but to be able to die well is indeed the highest wisdom of life. (*TDIO*, 76)

E

Henri Nouwen once stated that "the first and foremost task is faithfully to care for the inner fire." Kierkegaard would concur. The chief task, he would say, is to acquire earnestness. For it is only when we have earnestness that we can truly live. Without earnestness, dull repetition sets in. Anticipation of new possibilities disappears. Dreariness replaces vivacity.

This earnestness for Kierkegaard is not a brief kindling of fire on Sunday mornings. It is not a flare-up fueled by momentary passion. Intense passion blinds us to the value of a calm and persistent passion. It makes us think that the only passion worth having is fierce and furious. When Kierkegaard said that faith is the highest passion, he did not mean that it is a high-pitched concern that we should try to experience as often as we can (which in any case we cannot). He meant that it is a boundless interest that endures despite a day's ups and downs.

With this interest we will read the Bible as if it is about us personally. We will be aware that we will die, and with this awareness will gain life. We will be honest with ourselves so that we can uncover evasions and move toward single-minded motives.

Earnestness bestows vitality on our routines so that they no longer are dull repetitions. It awakens us to new possibilities, which gives us anticipation (or "expectancy") of things to come. Its vivacity dispels dreariness.

It is one thing, however, to know that the inner fire needs tending and another to know how to tend it. Kierkegaard doesn't say much about how we can acquire earnestness. He may have supposed that it will come once we are aware of the need for it or that we can simply choose to be earnest. There may be some truth to these suppositions, but not much. Ancient Christians felt the need to practice the disciplines of being silent, praying, reading scripture, and fasting. Many others have found that they need to be part of a community of faith to keep faith alive. (Kierkegaard wrote a good deal about how being in a community deadens faith, but nothing about how it enlivens faith.) It seems clear that in addition to knowing that earnestness is important, we will have to discover ways to keep it strong.

~

EARNESTNESS

When you read God's Word, in everything you read, continually to say to yourself: It is I to whom it is speaking, it is I about whom it is speaking—this is earnestness, precisely this is earnestness. (*FSE*, 36)

To be wide awake and to think death, to think what surely is more decisive than old age, which of course also has its time, to think that all was over, that everything was lost along with life, in order then to win everything in life—this is earnestness. (*TDIO*, 76)

Earnestness is precisely this kind of honest distrust of oneself, to treat oneself as a suspicious character. (*FSE*, 44)

EASY AND DIFFICULT

The easiness of Christianity is distinguished by one thing only: by the difficulty. Thus its yoke is easy and its burden light—for the person who has cast off all his burdens, all of them, the burdens of hope and of fear and of despondency and of despair—but it is very difficult. (*CUP*, I, 430)

THE ELEVENTH HOUR

In the eleventh hour one understands life quite differently than in the days of youth or in adulthood's busy time or in the final moment of old age. The person who repents at any other hour of the day repents temporally; he fortifies himself with a false and superficial notion of the insignificance of guilt; he fortifies himself with a deceptive and busy notion of the length of life—that person's regret is not in true inwardness. O eleventh hour, how changed everything is when you are present; how still everything is, as if it were the midnight hour; how earnest everything is, as if it were the hour of death; how solitary, as if it were among the tombstones; how solemn, as if it were in eternity! (*UDVS*, 15)

ENEMY

When a person struggles with the future, he learns that however strong he is otherwise, there is one enemy that is stronger—himself; there is one enemy he cannot conquer by himself, and that is himself. (*EUD*, 18)

ETERNITY

Not to be forgotten in the course of time was the lot of very few people, but something more glorious, not to be forgotten in eternity, is given to every human being who himself wills it. (*EUD*, 211)

EVASION

All this interpreting and interpreting and scholarly research and new scholarly research that is produced on the solemn and serious principle that it is in order to understand God's Word properly—look more closely and you will see that it is in order to defend oneself against God's Word. It is only all too easy to understand the requirement contained in God's Word. (*FSE*, 34)

All of us human beings are more or less intoxicated. But we are like a drunk man who is not completely drunk so that he has lost his consciousness—no, he is definitely conscious that he is a little drunk and for that very reason is careful to conceal it from others, if possible from himself. What does he do then? He looks for something to sustain himself; he walks close to the buildings and walks erect without becoming dizzy—a sober man. But he would not dare to cross a large square, because then what he himself knows full well would become obvious—that he is intoxicated. This is how it is, spiritually understood, with us human beings. We have a suspicion about ourselves; we gradually become conscious that we are not really sober. But then sagacity and sensibleness and levelheadedness come to our aid and with their help we obtain something to sustain us—the finite. And then we walk, erect and confident, without staggering—we are completely sober. But if the unconditioned unconditionally were to catch sight of us—yet we avoid this glance, and that is why we conceal ourselves in finitude and among the finitudes in the same way as Adam hid among the trees. (*JFY,* 113)

Quarrelling with people about what Christianity is is a mistake, for with very few exceptions their tactics aim at warding off understanding or learning what Christianity is, because they suspect that it is rather easy to grasp, but also that it would interfere with their lives. (*D,* 166)

The most pernicious of all evasions is—hidden in the crowd, to want, as it were, to avoid God's inspection of oneself as a single individual, avoid hearing God's voice as a single individual, as Adam once did when his bad conscience fooled him into thinking that he could hide among the trees. (*UDVS,* 128)

EXPECTANCY

In one's youth a person has plenty of expectation and possibility; they develop by themselves in the youth just like the precious myrrh that drips down from the trees of Arabia. But when a person has become older, his life usually remains what it has now become, a dull repetition and paraphrasing of the same old thing; no possibility awakeningly frightens; no possibility rejuvenatingly enlivens. Hope becomes something that belongs nowhere, and possibility something just as rare as green in winter. (*WL*, 250–51)

THE EXTERNAL PERSON

Most people live in the opposite way. They are busy with being something when someone is watching them. If possible, they are something in their own eyes as soon as others are watching them, but inwardly, where the absolute requirement is watching them, they have no taste for accentuating the personal *I*. (*CUP*, I, 503)

F

"Fear and trembling" may be the phrase that is most commonly associated with Kierkegaard. In his book with this title, he retells the story of Abraham taking his son Isaac up Mount Moriah to obey God's command to sacrifice Isaac. Abraham undoubtedly became fearful as he proceeded up the mountain. Even if he believed that God would provide a ram for the sacrifice, he must have felt more anguish with every step.

Kierkegaard may have used this story to illustrate what real faith is like. But the obvious question is how faith can coexist with fear and trembling. Is not faith sure and confident, the antithesis of trembling? How can it be fearful?

Kierkegaard gives us part of the answer when he says that fear and trembling are signs that we are constantly in process. If they are not present, we can easily be too sure of ourselves; and if we are too sure of ourselves, we can easily become stagnant and inert. Faith needs to be worked at to be kept alive. So fear and trembling are needed to keep faith vital.

To this thought we may add that fear and trembling also signify that we are not relying only on ourselves, but also on God. We do not trust ourselves to do or desire the good. We do not trust ourselves for salvation. We do not even trust ourselves to have faith.

We are faced, then, with a tension, for genuine faith seems also to be as secure and certain as the trust of a young child. This tension, however, is not a contradiction or an impossible conjoining of opposites. It says, "I trust, but with fear and trembling. I believe, but am still coming to believe."

If this conjoining is right, then faith must be accompanied with anxiety—not an anxiety that undermines faith, but one that moves it along.

∼

FAITH

One person can do much for another, but he cannot give him faith. (*EUD*, 12)

It was different in those ancient days. Faith was then a task for a whole lifetime, because it was assumed that proficiency in believing is not acquired either in days or in weeks. When the tried and tested oldster approached his end, had fought the good fight and kept the faith, his heart was still young enough not to have forgotten the anxiety and trembling that disciplined the youth, that the adult learned to control, but that no man outgrows. (*FT*, 7)

No one has the right to lead others to believe that faith is something inferior or that it is an easy matter, since on the contrary it is the greatest and most difficult of all. (*FT*, 52)

Faith ought not . . . to be made into something else to enable one to have it, but one ought rather to admit to not having it. (*FT*, 56)

Faith is the highest passion in a person. (*FT,* 122)

Faith is spontaneity after reflection. (*JP,* V, 447)

FALSE APPEARANCES

Weeds sometimes bear magnificent flowers. (*EUD,* 366)

FALSE VIRTUE

The person who does not know life's dangers—his courage is only a scarcely praiseworthy foolhardiness, and the person who does not know life's deceit—his expectancy is only an intoxication in dreams. (*EUD,* 212)

FEAR

The religious individual's fear is precisely fear for himself; the religious healing consists first and foremost in arousing this fear. (*SLW,* 468)

FEAR AND TREMBLING

Every human being is to live in fear and trembling, and likewise no established order is to be exempted from fear and trembling. Fear and trembling signify that we are in the process of becoming; and every single individual, likewise the generation, is and should be aware of being in the process of becoming. (*PC,* 88)

FEAR OF SHAME

If a person fears the shame of being caught in an error, not the error itself, then he is so far from being helped out of the error by this fear that he is led into something more corrupting—even if in other respects he was not in error. (*UDVS*, 45)

FINDING ONE'S NEIGHBOR

To choose a beloved, to find a friend, yes, this is a complicated business, but one's neighbor is easy to recognize, easy to find if only one will personally—acknowledge one's duty. (*WL*, 22)

FIRE

The brief kindling of the fire for an hour on Sundays only leaves one the more sluggish and slothful afterwards. (*D*, 118)

FOCUS

If you perceive that the pleasures of the world captivate you, and you wish to forget; if you perceive that earthly concerns occupy you so much that you wish to forget; if you perceive that life's busyness is carrying you away as the current carries the swimmer, and you wish to forget; if the anxieties of temptation pursue you and you fervently wish to be able to forget—then remember him, the Lord Jesus Christ, and you will certainly succeed. (*PC*, 153)

FORFEITING LOVE

In temporality a person perhaps can succeed in being able to dispense with love; he perhaps can succeed in slipping through time without discovering the self-deception; he perhaps can succeed, how terrible, in becoming, in a delusion, proud of being in it—but in eternity he cannot dispense with love and cannot avoid discovering that he forfeited everything. (*WL*, 6)

FORGIVENESS

When the sinner despairs of the forgiveness of sins, it is almost as if he walked right up to God and said, "No, there is no forgiveness of sins, it is impossible." (*SUD*, 114)

The eternal consolation in the doctrine of the forgiveness of sins is this: You shall believe it. For when the anxious conscience begins with heavy thoughts, and it is as if they could never in all eternity be forgotten, then comes this: You shall forget. You *shall* stop thinking of your sin. Not only are you permitted to let it alone, not only do you dare pray God for permission to dare forget—no, you shall forget, for you shall believe that your sins are forgiven. (*JP*, II, 49)

FRAILTY

A human being is a frail creature, not able like the God-man to know everything in advance, from the first moment, his suffering and the certainty and necessity of his downfall, and yet capable of living day after day, quiet, devoted to God, as if only everything good were in store for him. A human being must be handled gently, and that is why a person is given his task little by little; he is little by little pressed more and more firmly into the greater and greater effort of the test and examination. (*PC*, 186)

FRIENDS

Tell someone who your friends are, and he will know you. (*EUD*, 253)

G

Readers of Kierkegaard may wonder whether he believed in God's grace. Because so much of what he wrote aims at showing how hard it is to have genuine faith, it is difficult to see how he thinks grace fits into the Christian life. His emphasis on the necessity of working at one's faith and on the high ideals of New Testament Christianity do not seem to leave room for grace.

One consideration here is that the audience to whom Kierkegaard is writing is people in the Danish church. It is not atheists or those who are unacquainted with Christianity. His audience, in fact, officially believe in grace. It would not do, therefore, for him to preach grace to them. They would simply reply, "We believe in that!" What Kierkegaard must do is talk about grace indirectly so as to get those who think they believe in it really to believe in it.

In addition, Kierkegaard mentions grace now and then in his writings—rarely, to be sure, but definitely and affirmatively. In one of his journals, he writes, "No amount of striving can earn salvation. Therefore there is grace."

Last, Kierkegaard wants to rebut the assumption that taking in God's grace is easy. God's grace may be free, but it is nevertheless difficult to let this free gift sink into the deep parts of the personality. There is where the desires that prompt us, the basic projects we pursue, and the ambitions that lure us, reside. If we thought about the drives that really move us, we would see that grace does not accord well with them. We would see that if we took in grace deeply, it would force out these drives. And we shrink from this. Christianity, Kierkegaard declares in *Practice in Christianity,* "has been taken in vain, made too mild, so that people have forgotten what grace is; the more rigorous it is, the more grace becomes manifest as grace and not a sort of human sympathy" (274).

~

GAINING FAITH

In the last judgment, the question will surely be: Have you employed life to test whether you have faith or not, in order then to gain it? (*JP,* III, 539)

GENERALITY

General discussion of general truths can certainly give a person much to remember and can develop his understanding, but it is of only very little benefit to him. . . . Above all, generality is not for upbuilding, because one is never built up in general, any more than a house is erected in general. (*EUD,* 276)

GENTLE COURAGE

There is courage, which bravely defies dangers; there is high-mindedness, which proudly lifts itself above grievances; there is patience, which patiently bears sufferings; but the gentle courage that carries the heavy burden lightly is still the most wonderful compound. It is not wonderful with iron strength to deal harshly with what is the hardest of all, but it is wonderful to have iron strength and be able to deal gently with what is weakest of all, or deal lightly with what is heavy. (*UDVS*, 239–40)

THE GOOD

The good, the truly great and noble, is, of course, not just something general and as such the general object of knowledge; it is also something particular in relation to the individual's particular talent, so that one person is capable of more than another, so that one person is capable of it in one way, another in another. (*EUD*, 358)

THE GOOD AND THE EVIL

It is not only in the external world that God lets his light fall upon the good and the evil, his sun shine upon the just and the unjust—no, every Sabbath in his Church he lets his benediction shine upon the good and the evil. (*JP*, II, 92)

GRACE

The more one does his best to do good works with the idea of becoming saved, all the more anxious does he become, and his life becomes sheer self-torment. Far happier is the sinner who sighs briefly and to the point, "God be merciful to me, a sinner." (*JP*, II, 173)

The grace of God is indeed the most glorious of all. We certainly shall not dispute about that, since basically this is every human being's deepest and most blessed conviction. But very seldom does he think about it. . . . If he were to think the thought in its eternal validity, it would promptly aim a fatal blow at all his worldly thinking, aspiring, and pursuing, turn everything upside down for him, and this he cannot long endure. (*EUD*, 300)

GRATITUDE AND COMPASSION

Bernard says: Ingratitude dries up the springs of compassion, but Savonarola adds: Gratitude opens them. (*JP*, II, 190)

THE GREATEST DANGER TO CHRISTIANITY

The greatest danger to Christianity is, I contend, not heresies, heterodoxies, not atheists, not profane secularism—no, but the kind of orthodoxy which is cordial drivel, mediocrity served up sweet. (*JP*, III, 120)

GREATNESS

It is not what happens to me that makes me great but what I do. (*FT*, 64)

True greatness is equally accessible to all. (*FT*, 81)

GUILT AND PUNISHMENT

It is deeply rooted in human nature that guilt requires punishment. (*CUP*, I, 549)

H

In his novel *The Power and the Glory*, Graham Greene writes, "God might forgive cowardice and passion, but was it possible to forgive the habit of piety? He [the hunted priest] remembered the woman in the prison and how impossible it had been to shake her complacency." Not even God could puncture complacency, the priest thinks: "Salvation could strike like lightning at the evil heart, but the habit of piety excluded everything."

Kierkegaard would concur with this negative assessment of habit. Habit is a cunning enemy of faith, for one is not aware that habit undermines faith. One is not even aware that one has a habit. One just engages in unthinking repetition, which dulls one to the passion of faith.

Matters are not so clean-cut, however. For habit can also be a source of passionate faith. The simple repetition of faith-like actions can nurture faith. The phenomenon operates in a number of situations. A young child whose bedtime ritual involves being tucked in and kissed by a parent will come to love her parents. A parent who writes weekly to a child will come to look forward to his writing sessions. And one who regularly opens her Bible will anticipate her times with it.

Habits such as these often produce good memories, and the memories awake desire and fervor. These habits also produce a sense of stability, which nourishes enduring passion.

So the habit of piety has two forms, one that dulls and one that enlivens. Instead of simply wanting to replace habit with passion, we should want to replace dulling habits with enlivening ones. Though Kierkegaard is right to critique habit, we should not assume that the remedy is always to get rid of habit.

~

HABIT

Alas, of all enemies, habit is perhaps the most cunning, and above all it is cunning enough never to let itself be seen, because the person who sees the habit is saved from the habit. (*WL*, 36)

HARD ROAD

A person who has never made a beginning at willing the good is perhaps rarely to be found, but most people fall away when it is apparent that the road becomes harder instead of easier. (*UDVS*, 297)

HIDDEN PRIDE

Wanting to preach comfort to others but refusing to let oneself be comforted . . . is hidden pride. (*UDVS*, 36)

HINDSIGHT

The sad things about us human beings is really that in almost everything in our lives hindsight is best; that is, after we have done something, often badly, then we know how we should have done it. (*JP*, I, 469)

HONESTY

No person is saved except by grace; the apostle, too, was accepted only by grace. But there is one sin that makes grace impossible, that is dishonesty; and there is one thing God unconditionally must require, that is honesty. (*CD*, 187)

HOW

There is no work, not one single one, not even the best, about which we unconditionally dare to say: The one who does this unconditionally demonstrates love by it. It depends on *how* the work is done. (*WL*, 13)

THE HUMAN HEART

Oh, there is nothing as deceitful and as cunning as a human heart, resourceful in seeking escapes and finding excuses; and there surely is nothing as difficult and as rare as genuine honesty before God. (*CD*, 185)

HUNGER FOR WEALTH

There has never lived a rich pagan who has obtained *enough*. No, there is no hunger as insatiable as abundance's unnatural hunger. (*CD*, 35)

HYPOCRISY

The best defense against hypocrisy is love. (*WL*, 15)

I

Imagination is also something to beware of. We can picture ourselves having passionate faith or earnest love, and then through a trick of the imagination that we do not notice, turn the picture into a belief that we actually possess these. As Kierkegaard so succinctly put it, "A person can have imaginary feeling." What he meant was that we can imagine ourselves having certain feelings without distinguishing this imagining from actually having them. The reality, however, is that the feeling is not present, though we imagine it is.

As we have seen, Kierkegaard's focus in his writings is on the way in which our identifying with a community of faith makes us imagine that we have faith. Leo Tolstoy noticed the same phenomenon. "Quite often," he writes of himself in *Confession*, "a man goes on for years imagining that the religious teaching that had been imparted to him since childhood is still intact, while all the time there is not a trace of it left in him."

But as with habit, imagination is also something to cultivate. If we hold an image in our minds of what we want to be, we can let it draw us to the reality it represents. We can, for example, imagine ourselves speaking gently to someone who has hurt us. And we can resolve that when we next encounter this hurtful person we will act as we have imagined ourselves acting. Kierkegaard's example is of imagining the love of Jesus. By keeping this image in mind, we endow it with the power to draw us to a similar love. In this way, imagination can transform us.

Graham Greene described this ability in *The Power and the Glory.* "When you visualized a man or woman carefully, you could always begin to feel pity . . . that was a quality God's image carried with it . . . when you saw the lines at the corners of the eyes, the shape of the mouth, how the hair grew, it was impossible to hate. Hate was just a failure of imagination."

~

IDEALISM

To be an idealist in imagination is not at all difficult, but to have to *exist* as an idealist is an extremely rigorous life-task. (*CUP,* I, 353)

IDEALS

Ordinarily, most people aim their ideals at the Great, the Extraordinary, which they never attain. (*D,* 51)

IMAGINATION

A person can have imaginary feeling, knowing, and willing. (*SUD,* 30)

Let us imagine a youth. He looks and looks so long at this image [of the one who is on high] by which he feels himself drawn until the image becomes his one and only thought. The youth, we assume, has heard the story of the life that this uplifted one led in abasement and lowliness here on earth. We assume that the youth is not to be called light-minded, that accordingly he even makes every possible effort to visualize this suffering with the aid of his imagination. . . .

So the youth goes out into the world with this image before his eyes. . . . And it exercises its power over him, the power of love, which is indeed capable of everything, above all of making alike; his whole deepest inner being is transformed little by little, and he seems to be beginning to resemble, however imperfectly, this image that has made him forget everything—also the world in which he is, which now regards him with astonishment and alienation. (*PC*, 192–93)

IMMORTALITY

There ought not to be a question about immortality, whether there is an immortality, but the question ought to be whether I am living in such a way as my immortality requires of me. There ought not to be discussion about immortality, whether there is an immortality, but about what my immortality requires of me, about my enormous responsibility in my being immortal. (*CD*, 205)

IMPERSONALITY

If God's Word is for you merely a doctrine, something impersonal and objective, then it is no mirror—an objective doctrine cannot be called a mirror; it is just as impossible to look at yourself in an objective doctrine as to look at yourself in a wall. (*FSE*, 43–44)

IN THE LIVING ROOM

It is in the living room that the battle must be fought, not imaginatively in church, with the pastor shadowboxing and the listeners looking on.... If the pastor's activity in the church is merely a once-a-week attempt to tow the congregation's cargo ship a little closer to eternity, the whole thing comes to nothing, because a human life, unlike a cargo ship, cannot lie in the same place until the next Sunday. (*CUP*, I, 465)

INDIFFERENCE

If anyone thinks he has faith and yet is indifferent toward this possession, is neither cold nor hot, he can be certain that he does not have faith. If anyone thinks he is a Christian and yet is indifferent toward being that, then he really is not one at all. Indeed, what would we think of a person who gave assurances that he was in love and also that it was a matter of indifference to him? (*WL*, 26–27)

INFLUENCE

To come in the name of the king opens every door for a person, but to come in God's name is the last thing he should try; and the person who must be contented with that must be contented with little. (*EUD*, 301)

INTEREST IN THE GOOD

Besides all its other good qualities, the good, the truly great and noble, has the quality of not allowing the observer to be indifferent. It elicits a pledge, as it were, from the person who has once caught a vision of it. However deep that person sinks, he never actually forgets it completely. (*EUD*, 359)

J–K

"I wish to make people aware, so that they do not squander and dissipate their lives," Kierkegaard once wrote in his journals. The kind of awareness he had in mind is largely awareness of ourselves—the hidden motives that move us, the sly and crafty ways we evade the good, the ulterior inducements that bring about imitation compassion. If we are not aware of these, Kierkegaard seems to be assuming, we will be ruled by them. And this means that our lives will be squandered and dissipated—we will not be purposeful in what we do; we will not pursue the good for the sake of the good; we will not even have before us the pure and unadulterated idea of the good.

We might wonder, though, whether the assumption is correct. Will we be ruled by hidden motives, crafty evasions, and ulterior inducements if we have no self-awareness? Why cannot we simply love and be compassionate without wondering whether we are motivated by unsavory motives? Must we be as suspicious of ourselves as Kierkegaard apparently wants us to be?

Kierkegaard was aware of these questions and seems to have allowed for those who simply and genuinely do what is good without the awareness he wants to incite. He writes in *Upbuilding Discourses in Various Spirit,* "The sagacious person needs to take a lot of time and trouble to understand what the simple person at the joyous prompting of a pious heart feels no need to understand in lengthy detail, because he at once simply understands only the good" (25).

The trouble, however, with assuming that we are such simple souls is that it might not be so. We might think we seize the good immediately when in fact we are moved by precisely the hidden motives, evasions, and inducements that Kierkegaard wants us to be aware of. In fact, chances are that we are not so simple as we want to believe. Most of us have so much stirring underneath our everyday conscious- ness that we need to probe and poke, uncover and unveil—in other words, do the self-analysis that Kierkegaard's writings provoke us to. Our aim, to be sure, is the same as that of the simple soul—to seize the good immediately—but the process of getting there is a good deal more demanding and agonizing.

∾

JUDGING

Woe to him who wants to judge hearts. (*CUP*, I, 587)

KNOCKING AT THE DOOR

It is eternally true that if one knocks, the door will be opened. But suppose that the difficulty for us human beings is simply that we are afraid to go—and knock. (*JP*, II, 22)

KNOWING AND DOING

To understand is a pleasure, also this, to understand, to know how sly and crafty we human beings are, how we all know how to talk about the good; no cultured person would put up with being thought ignorant of it, with being thought personally unable to describe it profoundly and eloquently, because to understand, also the secrets of subtlety, is a pleasure. But personally to strive to be the honest, upright, and unselfish one—no, that would indeed be an effort. (*JFY,* 115)

We human beings, sly as always with regard to God and divine truth, have directed all our attention to understanding, to knowing. We make out as if the difficulty were there and as if it would follow naturally that if we only understand the right it follows automatically that we do it. What a grievous misunderstanding or what a sly fabrication! (*JFY,* 115–16)

In every human being there is a capacity, the capacity for knowledge. And every person—the most knowing and the most limited—is in his knowing far beyond what he is in his life or what his life expresses. Yet this misrelation is of little concern to us. On the contrary, we set a high price on knowledge, and everyone strives to develop his knowing more and more. . . . There is nothing more deceitful than the human heart, and this perhaps never appears more clearly than in this misrelation between our understanding and our acting. If this is judged very rigorously, the charge would have to be that we are all hypocrites. (*JFY,* 118–19)

KNOWING GOD

The majority of people live far too securely in life and therefore get to know God so little. (*JP*, V, 361)

KNOWING ONESELF BEFORE GOD

If self-knowledge does not lead to knowing oneself before God—well, then there is something to what purely human self-observation says, namely, that this self-knowledge leads to a certain emptiness that produces dizziness. Only by being before God can one totally come to oneself. (*JFY*, 106)

L

Sprinkled throughout Kierkegaard's intense thoughts and sometimes rather dark musings are lyrical and uplifting passages. These passages are just as insightful and thought-provoking as the others, but they hold the reader in their embrace because of their elegance and charm. One of them occurs at the end of "Love Hides a Multitude of Sins" in *Works of Love:* "How often has not the anger that smoldered within, only waiting for an occasion, how often has it not been smothered because loved gave no occasion! . . . Oh, have not many crimes been averted, many evil intentions frustrated, many desperate resolutions consigned to oblivion, many sinful thoughts halted on the way to becoming action, many rash words suppressed in time because love did not give the occasion!" (299)

Another occurs in the middle of the first essay titled "Love Will Hide a Multitude of Sins" in *Eighteen Upbuilding Discourses.* If an appetite for sin lives in our heart, Kierkegaard says, we will discover numerous sins in others. But "when love lives in the heart, the eye is shut and does not discover the open act of sin" (60). If we are rash, we will not take the time to look into the context of what we have heard someone say and will be likely to give it the worst interpretation. But "when love lives in the heart, a person understands slowly and does not hear at all words said in haste and does not understand them when repeated because he assigns them a good position and a good meaning" (60–61).

A third occurs in "The Invitation" in *Practice in Christianity*. The invitation is, "Come here, all you who labor and are burdened, and I will give you rest." The invitation "goes out, and wherever there is a crossroad, it stands still and calls. . . . It stands at the crossroad, there where temporal and earthly suffering placed its cross, and calls. Come here, all you poor and wretched, you who must slave in poverty to secure for yourselves—not a carefree but a hard future. . . .Come here, all you sorrowing ones, you who, burdened, labor in futility! . . . Come here, all, all, all of you; with him is rest. And he makes no difficulty; he does only one thing: he opens his arms" (16–19).

∾

LIKE OTHERS

The situation is this. If everyone around defines himself as being a Christian *just like* "the others," then no one, if it is looked at this way, is really confessing Christ. (*PC*, 219)

LIVING

It is quite true what Philosophy says: that Life must be understood backwards. But that makes one forget the other saying: that it must be lived—forwards. (*D*, 111)

The easiest thing of all is to die; the difficult thing is to live. (*JP*, II, 165)

LIVING IN THE PRESENT

A life of a human being begins with the illusion that a long, long time and a whole world lie before him in the distance, begins with the foolhardy delusion that he has such ample time for his many claims. . . . But when a person in the infinite transformation discovers the eternal itself so close to life that there is not the distance of one single claim, of one single evasion, of one single excuse, of one single moment of time from what *he* in this instant, in this second, in this holy moment *shall* do—then he is on the way to becoming a Christian. (*WL*, 90)

LONGING FOR GOD

The wind blows where it will; you are aware of its soughing, but no one knows whence it comes or whither it goes. So also with longing, the longing for God and the eternal, the longing for our Savior and Redeemer. Comprehend it you cannot, nor should you; indeed, you dare not even want to attempt it—but you are to use the longing. Would the merchant be responsible if he does not use the opportune moment; would the sailor be responsible if he does not use the favorable wind—how much more, then, is the one who does not use the occasion of longing when it is offered. (*CD*, 253)

LOSING ONESELF

The greatest hazard of all, losing the self, can occur very quietly in the world, as if it were nothing at all. No other loss can occur so quietly; any other loss—an arm, a leg, five dollars, a wife, etc.—is sure to be noticed. (*SUD*, 32–33)

LOSING ONE'S SOUL

If someone lost his earthly treasure, it still would be lost only for this life, . . . death would . . . reconcile him to the loss and remove it from him when in the moment of death he became like one who previously had not lost anything. But if he lost his soul, it would be lost for all time and for eternity; . . . death would be unable to help him. (*EUD*, 186)

LOUD TALK

Ah, it gets so turned around! We think that religiousness, instead of being a matter of every individual's going alone into his private room to talk softly with himself, is a matter of talking very loudly. (*JP*, II, 397)

LOVE

What is it that is never changed even though everything is changed? It is love. And only that which never becomes something else is love, that which gives away *everything* and *for that reason* demands nothing, that which demands nothing and therefore has nothing to lose, that which blesses and blesses when it is cursed, that which loves its neighbor but whose enemy is also its neighbor, that which leaves revenge to the Lord because it takes comfort in the thought that he is even more merciful. (*EUD*, 56–57)

Just as there is a power in sin that has the perseverance to consume every better feeling a person has, so there is a heavenly power that starves the multiplicity of sin out of a person—this power is the love that hides a multitude of sins. (*EUD*, 64)

The person who thinks of his own perfection does not love, and he who takes his own imperfections into account does not love. (*EUD*, 74)

It is a sad but altogether too common inversion to go on talking continually about how the object of love must be so it can be loveworthy, instead of talking about how love must be so it can be love. (*WL*, 159)

LOVE AND CONFIDENCE

We like to be near someone who loves, because he casts out fear. Whereas the mistrustful person scares everyone away, whereas the crafty and cunning spread anxiety and painful disquietude around them, whereas the presence of a domineering person is as oppressive as the heavy pressure of sultry air—love gives bold confidence. (*WL*, 280–81)

LOVE AND SUFFERING

One always loves more something for which one has suffered. (*PC*, 191)

LOVE AND UNDERSTANDING

Only the person who loves him [Christ] understands that he was love, and therefore only he can become aware of how he suffered: how severely, how agonizingly, and how he suffered: how gently, how lovingly, how he suffered: how right he was, how he suffered—what wrong! If this sight does not move you in this way, then it must be because you do not love him. (*PC*, 178–79)

Surrounded by hordes of men, absorbed in all sorts of secular matters, more and more shrewd about the ways of the world—such a person forgets himself, forgets his name divinely understood, does not dare to believe in himself, finds it too hazardous to be himself and far easier and safer to be like the others, to become a copy, a number, a mass man. (*SUD*, 33–34)

LOVE OF ENEMIES

People think that it is impossible for a human being to love his enemy, because, alas, enemies are hardly able to endure the sight of one another. Well, then, shut your eyes—then the enemy looks just like the neighbor. (*WL*, 68)

LOVE OF FAULTS

It is only all too certain that every human being, unfortunately, has a great inclination to see his neighbor's faults and perhaps an even greater one to want to tell them. (*WL*, 290)

LOVE OF ONESELF

The commandment said, "You shall love your neighbor as yourself," but if the commandment is properly understood it also says the opposite: *You shall love yourself in the right way.* Therefore, if anyone is unwilling to learn from Christianity to love himself in the right way, he cannot love the neighbor either. (*WL,* 22)

LOVE OF THE SHABBY

This is the remarkable thing: if someone has discovered how fundamentally good-natured almost every human being is, he would hardly dare to acknowledge his discovery, and he would fear becoming ludicrous, perhaps even fear that humanity would feel insulted by it. If, however, someone pretends that he had discovered how fundamentally shabby every human being is, how envious, how selfish, how faithless, and what abomination can lie hidden in the purest, that is, in the one regarded by simpletons and silly geese and small-town beauties as the purest—that person conceitedly knows that he is welcome, that it is the yield of his observing, his knowledge, his story that the world longs to hear. (*WL,* 284)

LOVING THE WEAK

The sagacious person thinks, foolishly, that one wastes one's love by loving imperfect, weak people; I should think that this is applying one's love, making use of it. (*WL,* 163)

LUST

There is something very profound in the stories about the Mount of Venus, that the person who went there was not able to find the way back. It is always difficult to find the way back from lust. (*JP*, IV, 289)

M

"Can you think of anything more appalling than having it all end with the disintegration of your essence into a multiplicity?" Kierkegaard asks. The question seems esoteric. Is there something in it to which the ordinary person can relate?

There is. It is that a basic human drive is to be single-minded, to have a central focus. Put negatively, we do not want to be pulled in opposite directions. If we were, we would feel that we were disintegrating. We want our personalities to have a fundamental harmony.

The desire for harmony does not mean that we do not want to have different interests. We do. We want a rich and expansive life, filled with numerous activities, some of which are very different from others.

What the desire for harmony means is that we do not want to go in opposite directions with respect to fundamental concerns. We do not want both to love and hate the good. If we are persons of faith, we want to be rid of skepticism and doubt. If we did go in opposite directions with respect to these fundamental concerns, we would be a multiplicity from which we would shrink with consternation and dismay.

The plain fact, however, is that we are multiplicities in this sense. The Apostle Paul wrote that "I find it to be a law that when I want to do what is good, evil lies close at hand" (Romans 7:21). Augustine confessed, "I was neither wholly willing nor wholly unwilling" (*Confessions*, Book 8, Section 10), meaning that he was both willing and unwilling, but not wholly either. And in *Purity of Heart Is to Will One Thing*, Kierkegaard described in agonizing detail a number of ways in which we are both willing and unwilling. We are attracted to the good, he said, but not completely, and we also defy the good, but again not completely.

The aim for Paul, Augustine, and Kierkegaard is to desire the good and only the good. When we do, we will, to use Kierkegaard's phrase, acquire "the binding power of the personality." We will avoid being "several."

From one perspective, this aim is the most important goal we can have in life. When we acquire a central binding power, we will be willing the good and only the good. We will not be resisting it or willing it for ulterior reasons, and we will not possess other motives that obscure it.

∾

MEANING

If a human being did not have an eternal consciousness, if underlying everything there were only a wild, fermenting power that writhing in dark passions produced everything, be it significant or insignificant, if a vast, never appeased emptiness hid beneath everything, what would life be then but despair? (*FT*, 15)

THE MEMORY OF A DEATH

There is nothing that next to God himself so uncompromisingly tests and searches a person's innermost being as does a commemoration of one who is dead preserved in an always present memory. (*EUD*, 210)

MERCIFULNESS

It does not follow that because a person has a heart in his bosom he has money in his pocket, but the first is still more important and certainly is decisive with regard to mercifulness. Truly—if a person does not have money but knows how to encourage and inspire the poor, the miserable, by speaking about mercifulness—would he not do just as much as someone who throws some money to poverty or preaches charitable donations out of the rich man's pocket! (*WL*, 316)

MINOR EVENTS

The more unimportant something is, the more difficult it is to join the God-conception together with it. And yet it is right here that the relationship with God will be known. . . . Therefore one should not be fooled when a pastor omits the minor events of life and concentrates his eloquence and mimic art on great episodes, and at most half-ashamedly, for the sake of decency, adds at the end that also in the everyday life one ought to show the same faith, the same hope, and the same courage. (*CUP,* I, 487)

MITIGATING EXPLANATION

By a *mitigating explanation* the one who loves hides a multitude of sins. . . . It is always in my power, if I am one who loves, to choose the most lenient explanation. If, then, this more lenient or mitigating explanation explains what others light-mindedly, hastily, harshly, hardheartedly, enviously, maliciously, in short, unlovingly explain summarily as guilt, if the mitigating explanation explains this in another way, it removes now one and now another guilt and in this way reduces the multitude of sins or hides it. (*WL*, 291-92)

MULTIPLICITY

Can you think of anything more appalling than having it all end with the disintegration of your essence into a multiplicity, so that you actually became several, just as that unhappy demoniac became a legion, and thus you would have lost what is the most inward and holy in a human being, the binding power of the personality? (*EO*, Part II, 160)

MY SALVATION

They argue about whether God intends the salvation of all or only of some—almost forgetting the far more important theme: You, O God, intend my salvation; would that I myself might intend it also. (*JP*, IV, 530)

N

Pascal wrote that we contain an infinite abyss that can be filled only with "an infinite and immutable object; in other words by God himself" (*Pensees*, #148). C. S. Lewis refers to this abyss as a "God-shaped vacuum"—a place in the human heart that only God can fill. Both Pascal and Lewis lament that we try in vain to put everything else but God into the abyss. Pascal also laments that we evade knowing that we contain an abyss. If we knew about it, we would have to encounter God. But we would rather live as though we do not need God.

Kierkegaard mourns with Pascal and Lewis. We need God. "What matters," Kierkegaard said on his deathbed, "is to get as close to God as possible." But it is one thing to need God and another to recognize that we do. And not to recognize that we do is a tragedy worthy of sorrow and lamentation. For if we do not recognize our need for God, we will not try to satisfy it. The abyss will remain empty, or at least empty of the one thing that could fill it.

It is important to add that neither Pascal nor Kierkegaard would say that people are unaware of their need for God. That is, no one ever goes from birth to death without at some point sensing the presence of the abyss. This must be so or else it would make no sense to say that we hide the presence of the abyss from ourselves, or that we flee from God, or, to use Kierkegaard's words, that we are in defiance against God. If we flee from something, we must have at least a dim awareness of it.

So the situation is something like this. At times we are aware of our need for God, sometimes with full consciousness and sometimes with half consciousness. At other times, we suppress this awareness.

This situation is expressed picturesquely in the passage in the "L" section titled "Longing for God." The intermittent awareness of our need for God is like the coming and going of the wind. It is unpredictable and out of our control. When it comes, though, we should seize it.

∾

NEEDING GOD

It is the saddest thing of all if a human being goes through life without discovering that he needs God. (*EUD*, 303)

NEIGHBOR LOVE

The neighbor is not one who is more distinguished than you, since to love him because he is more distinguished can very easily be preference and to that extent self-love; neither is the neighbor one who is inferior to you, since to love him because he is inferior can very easily be the condescension of preference and to that extent self-love. No, to love the neighbor means equality. (*JP*, IV, 292)

NEVER LOVED

Who, indeed, has ever been more impoverished than someone who has never loved! (*WL*, 175)

THE NEXT DAY

If there is no next day for you, then all earthly care is annihilated. . . . When the next day comes, it loses its enchantment and its disquieting insecurity. If there is no next day for you, then either you are dying or you are one who by dying to temporality grasped the eternal, either one who is actually dying or one who is *really* living. . . . The one who rows a boat turns his back to the goal toward which he is working. So it is with the next day. When, with the help of the eternal, a person lives absorbed in today, he turns his back to the next day. The more he is eternally absorbed in today, the more decisively he turns his back to the next day; then he does not see it at all. (*CD*, 72–73)

NO SHORTCUT

There is no shortcut to the absolute good. . . . To chance upon it in an easier way (by being born in especially propitious years, for example, in the nineteenth century, by being very intelligent, by being born in the same town as a great man or being related by marriage to an apostle), to be a favorite of fortune, is merely evidence that one is duped. (*CUP*, I, 428)

O

Kierkegaard argued vigorously and repeatedly that faith cannot be purely objective. Faith is a passion, he declared, the highest passion. The word he used most to characterize faith is "subjectivity." A subjective relationship to God is both personal and concrete, which is what faith must be if it is to connect to God rightly. Objective knowledge of God, on the other hand, is impersonal and abstract. It has no inner connection to God except via concepts, which have no passion in them.

Why does Kierkegaard take such pains to point out the obvious difference between a subjective relationship to God and objective knowledge of God?

The point Kierkegaard wanted to make is that we use objective knowledge of God as a substitute for subjective faith. We do so, he says, in order to hide from God. The substitution is one of our clever evasive tactics—clever because we think that we are properly connected to God with objective knowledge, even though we are fully aware of the difference between it and subjective faith. And the substitution is one toward which we seem naturally to gravitate, or in Kierkegaard's words, is "a congenital genius we all have."

Kierkegaard is not rejecting objective knowledge of God, but pointing out that we have a proclivity to misuse it. He is saying that if all we have is objective knowledge of God, then we are without faith. "The one who has objective Christianity and nothing else is *eo ipso* [precisely thereby] a pagan, because Christianity is precisely a matter of spirit and of subjectivity and of inwardness" (*CUP,* I, 43). Kierkegaard does not say that a Christian has no objective knowledge of God, but that with only such knowledge and no earnestness ("objective Christianity and nothing else"), we will not have faith.

≈

OBJECTIONS TO CHRISTIANITY

It is claimed that arguments against Christianity arise out of doubt. This is a total misunderstanding. The arguments against Christianity arise out of insubordination, reluctance to obey, mutiny against all authority. Therefore, until now the battle against objections has been shadowboxing, because it has been intellectual combat with doubt instead of being ethical combat against mutiny. (*JP,* I, 359)

OBJECTIVITY

This impersonality (objectivity) in relation to God's Word is all too easy for us human beings to maintain; it is actually a congenital genius we all have, something we obtain gratis—by way of hereditary sin—since this praised impersonality (objectivity) is neither more nor less than a lack of conscience. (*FSE,* 40)

OBSERVING

It does not depend, then, merely upon what one sees, but what one sees depends upon how one sees; all observation is not just a receiving, a discovering, but also a bringing forth, and insofar as it is that, how the observer himself is constituted is indeed decisive. (*EUD*, 59)

OFFENSE

It is the New Testament's most definite statement—that Christianity and being a true Christian must to the highest degree be an offense to the natural man. . . . This is how Christianity, which is the qualification of *spirit*, must appear to anyone who has not, by dying to, been reborn to be *spirit*. (*JFY*, 140)

When Christianity came into the world, it did not itself need to point out (even though it did do so) that it was an offense, because the world, which took offense, certainly discovered this easily enough. But now, now when the world has become Christian, now Christianity above all must itself pay attention to the offense. (*WL*, 199)

OUR TASK

The task is to become a Christian or to continue to be a Christian, and the most dangerous illusion of all is to become so sure of being one that all Christendom must be defended against the Turk—instead of defending the faith within oneself against the illusion about the Turk. (*CUP*, I, 608)

P

Pascal wrote, "I can feel nothing but compassion for those who sincerely lament their doubt, who regard it as the ultimate misfortune, and who, sparing no effort to escape from it, make their search their principal and most serious business. But as for those who spend their lives without a thought for this final end of life . . . , I view them very differently. This negligence in a matter where they themselves, their eternity, their all are at stake, fills me more with irritation than pity; it astounds and appalls me." (*Pensees*, #427)

It appalled Kierkegaard as well. He wanted his readers to be passionate. And this, he thought, meant that they would be concerned about their ultimate fate. With "feeling, imagination, and inwardness," they would make it a priority to pursue what matters most.

Instead, people give up passion for trivialities. They are consumed with misplaced priorities. Their imaginations are occupied with trifling projects. They fill their day with frivolous activities. Their spare energy is spent in inconsequential pastimes.

Perhaps this indifference to what is significant prompted Plato to remark near the end of *The Republic*, "The struggle to be good or bad is important, my dear Glaucon," and then to add, "much more important than people think." Plato was astute enough to realize that people need to be reminded that there is a difference between the important and the trivial. They become so immersed in what is trivial that the sense of what matters fades. If, however, people could maintain their passion for the important, they would not be overtaken by the trivial.

~

PASSION AND TRIVIALITIES

Over the years, an individual may abandon the little bit of passion, feeling, imagination, the little bit of inwardness he had and embrace as a matter of course an understanding of life in terms of trivialities. (*SUD*, 59)

PATIENCE

Only impatience knows fear, but patience, like love, drives out fear. (*EUD*, 216)

POSSIBILITY AND ACTUALITY

In possibility Christianity is easy; and merely expounded, that is, kept in possibility, it pleases people. In actuality it is so difficult, and expressed in actuality, that is, as action, it incites people against you. . . . When you see a speaker who merely with some competence gives an exposition of Christianity, but no more than that, therefore in possibility—he becomes honored, esteemed, loved, almost idolized by people. How close at hand lies the conclusion that if now in addition his life expressed it, how beloved would he then be—ah, my dear fellow, let him beware of that! (*JFY,* 116–17)

All have their great moments, see themselves in the magic mirror of possibility that hope holds before them while desire flatters, but they speedily forget the vision in the everyday. (*UDVS,* 31)

It is a dangerous business to arrive in eternity with possibilities which one himself has prevented from becoming actualities. Possibility is a hint from God. A person must follow it. (*JP,* III, 535)

PRAYING

A person usually desires far too many things, lets his soul flutter with every breeze. But he who prays knows how to make distinctions; little by little he gives up that which according to his earthly conception is less important, since he does not really dare to come before God with it. (*EUD,* 393–94)

To pray is not to listen to oneself speak but is to become silent and to remain silent, to wait until the one praying hears God. (*WA,* 12)

PRESENT TO ONESELF

How rare is the person who actually is contemporary with himself; ordinarily most people are apocalyptically, in theatrical illusions, hundreds of thousands of miles ahead of themselves, or several generations ahead of themselves in feelings, in delusions, in intentions, in resolutions, in wishes, in longings. But the believer (the one present) is in the highest sense contemporary with himself. To be totally contemporary with oneself today with the help of the eternal is also the most formative and generative; it is the gaining of eternity. (*CD*, 74–75)

PRIDE

The proud, noble nature can bear everything, but one thing it cannot bear—it cannot bear sympathy. (*FT*, 104)

The proud person always wants to do the right thing, the great thing, and he is actually struggling not with people but with God, because he wants to do it with his own power; he does not want to sneak out of something—no, what he wants is to set the task as high as possible and then to finish it by himself, satisfied with his own consciousness and his own approval. (*EUD*, 354)

PRIORITIES

Oh, the concern about an eternal salvation turns the mind from all misplaced considerations! (*EUD*, 271)

PROOF OF CHRISTIANITY

The best proof for the immortality of the soul, that there is a God, and the like, is the impression one has of this from his childhood, and therefore this proof, unlike those numerous scholarly and high-sounding proofs, could be stated thus: It is absolutely certain, for my father told me. (*JP,* II, 31)

PSEUDO-LOVE

No doubt it rarely occurs to a person brazenly to speak ill of loving; far more common, however, is the deception by which people defraud themselves out of actually starting to love because they speak too fanatically about loving and about love. (*WL,* 161)

Q–R

Kierkegaard's analysis of the gradual eclipse of our "ethical and ethical-religious comprehension" in the selection under "Resistance" is extraordinarily astute. What he means by this phrase is something like, "knowing what is good," or "knowing how God wishes us to live." If we do not want to act in accordance with this knowing, Kierkegaard says, we do not normally simply go ahead and do the opposite. That is rare. Rather, we think about the matter for a bit. Gradually, our knowing dims. That is, the strength of our conviction about what is good lessens. We do not see it so clearly. Our desire to do the opposite begins to become stronger than the conviction. After some time has elapsed, the original conviction has disappeared entirely. It has been eclipsed by the opposite desire—the willing, as Kierkegaard calls it. So willing and knowing now concur. And in this way our first persuasion, which was right, is undone.

Part of Kierkegaard's point in this description of the undoing of our ethical and religious knowing is that resistance to what is good is seldom open and obvious. When we sin, we rarely do so knowing at the time that what we are doing is sin. This is because we have not held our initial knowing of the good clearly before our minds. And we have not done this because, at some point (though seldom), we have knowingly resisted doing so. Later, the memory of the resistance becomes clouded, so that we are prone to say that it was not in fact a knowing resistance. It gradually becomes deeply buried in a morass of beliefs and desires. But it is still there, operating on us from its unseen depths.

Reading this analysis in Kierkegaard prompts one to say with Augustine, "Who can untie this twisted mass of knots?" There is a good deal more to our ethical and religious personalities than meets the eye.

~

REAL VICTORY

It is one thing to let ideas compete with ideas, and it is one thing to argue and win in a dispute; it is something else to be victorious over one's own mind when one battles in the actuality of life. (*WL*, 78)

RECEIVING

It is better to give than to receive, but it can sometimes be more humble to be willing to receive than to be willing to give. Perhaps there has been someone who in love was prepared to give away everything but was not willing to receive anything. (*JP*, II, 45)

REPENTANCE

In the temporal and sensuous and civic sense, repentance is still also something that comes and goes over the years, but in the eternal sense it is a quiet daily concern. (*UDVS,* 18)

Of repentance it must be said that, if it is forgotten, then its strength was nothing but immaturity, but the longer and more deeply it is preserved, the better it becomes. (*UDVS,* 19)

RESISTANCE

If willing does not agree with what is known [to be right], then it does not necessarily follow that willing goes ahead and does the opposite of what knowing understood (presumably such strong opposites are rare); rather, willing allows some time to elapse, an interim called: "We shall look at it tomorrow." During all this, knowing becomes more and more obscure, and the lower nature gains the upper hand more and more. . . . Gradually, willing's objection to this development lessens; it almost appears to be in collusion. And when knowing has become duly obscured, knowing and willing can better understand each other; eventually they agree completely, for now knowing has come over to the side of willing and admits that what it wants is absolutely right. And this is how perhaps the great majority of men live: they work gradually at eclipsing their ethical and ethical-religious comprehension. (*SUD,* 94)

Most people . . . fear resistance from the outside, and do not know the horrible pain of inward resistance. (*D,* 58–59)

RESOLUTIONS

The devil uses many arts to tempt a human being, and it is always a dangerous assault when the devil, by means of high-minded resolutions, or rather by talk about them and admiration of them, together with the subsequent distaste when a person sees how little he can do, wants to induce him to give up everything. No, we creep before we learn to walk, and to want to fly is always precarious. To be sure, there are great decisions, but even in regard to them the main thing is to activate one's resolution, lest one become so high-flying in the resolution that one forgets to walk. (*EUD*, 348–49)

It really would not help a person (even if the one speaking were capable of it) if the speaker, by his oratorical artistry, led him to jump into a half hour's resolution, by the ardor of conviction started a fire in him so that he would blaze in a momentary good intention without being able, however, to sustain a resolution or to nourish an intention as soon as the speaker stopped talking. (*EUD*, 381)

RESTLESSNESS

Faith expressly signifies the deep, strong, blessed restlessness that drives the believer so that he cannot settle down at rest in this world, and therefore the person who has settled down completely at rest has also ceased to be a believer, because a believer cannot sit still as one sits with a pilgrim's staff in one's hand—a believer travels forward. (*UDVS*, 218)

RETREAT

Just as the first book in the Old Testament has been called Genesis, the second, Exodus, so it could very well be said that in human life there is a third book that is called Retreat. (*EUD*, 248)

REVENGE

Every human being, if he is honest, only all too often catches himself in being able, protractedly, penetratingly, and expertly, to interpret the sad truth that revenge is sweet. (*EUD*, 57)

S

The sensitive and vulnerable reader of Kierkegaard can easily become depressed. So much of what Kierkegaard writes is focused on the subtle ways we deceive ourselves that we may lose any hope of acquiring an uncorrupted faith. And such a large part of what he says deals with the dim secrets underlying conscious thought that we are liable to regard human nature as dark and shadowy, containing little good. This section is full of sayings that prompt these cheerless and disheartening reactions.

The truth is that though self-suspicion is necessary, it needs to be tempered with both a warning and an antidote. The warning is that too much self-suspicion can make us morose. Moroseness can lead to despair. And despair can undermine faith. Too much self-suspicion can also make us too critical of ourselves. Being too critical of ourselves can injure a proper self-love. And without a proper self-love, we will not be able to live well with ourselves. In addition, too much self-suspicion can make us critical of others. If all we ever find in ourselves is ulterior motives, we are likely to look at others with a faultfinding and deprecatory eye. We need, accordingly, to take self-suspicion in measured doses.

The antidote to too much self-suspicion is to look for goodness and beauty. It is to train ourselves to become aware of these, to become sensitive to their presence, to notice them in our acquaintances. It is also to revel in the goodness and beauty we notice, to take delight in them, and to relish them. Doing these will dispel the moroseness, despair, and belittling attitude provoked by too much self-suspicion.

In fairness to Kierkegaard, it needs to be pointed out that on occasion he depicts instances of goodness and beauty, as in the selection under "Scripture." But as in life itself, we can miss these occasions if we have become too immersed in uncovering questionable motives. We need to work at becoming more attuned to the beauty and goodness without becoming less aware of the motives.

~

SALVATION

Even our good deeds are nothing but human fabrications, fragile and very ambiguous, but every person has heaven's salvation only by the grace and mercy of God. (*EUD*, 271)

Holy Scripture teaches for our salvation that sin is a human being's corruption and therefore deliverance is only in purity through willing the good. (*UDVS*, 32)

SCRIPTURE

Every good and every perfect gift is from above and comes down from the Father of lights, with whom there is no change or shad-

ow of variation. These words are so beautiful, so appealing, so moving, they are so soothing and comforting, so simple and intelligible, so curative and healing. (*EUD*, 48)

SECRET ANXIETY

Deep within every person's soul there is a secret anxiety that even the one in whom he had the most faith could also become unfaithful to him. No merely human love can completely drive out this anxiety, which can very well remain hidden and undetected in the friendly security of a happy life-relationship, but which at times can inexplicably stir deep within and which, when the storms of life begin, is immediately at hand. There is only one whose faithfulness can drive out this anxiety, and that is Jesus Christ. (*CD*, 284)

SECRET MOTIVES

Ah, human sympathy, how often was it only curiosity, not sympathy, that made you dare to venture into a sufferer's secret. (*PC*, 21)

SEEING

When evil lives in the heart, the eye sees offense, but when purity lives in the heart, the eye sees the finger of God. (*EUD*, 60)

SELF-DECEPTION

The person who is deceived by the world can still hope that he will not be disappointed some other time under other circumstances, but the person who deceives himself is continually deceived even if he flees to the farthest limits of the world, because he cannot escape himself. (*EUD*, 211)

The world *wants* to be deceived. . . . Intensely, more intensely, more passionately perhaps than any witness to the truth has fought for the truth, the world fights to be deceived; it most gratefully rewards with applause, money, and prestige anyone who complies with its wish to be deceived. (*JFY*, 140–41)

SELF-FORGETFULNESS

The one who in love forgets himself, forgets his suffering, in order to think of someone else's, forgets all his misery in order to think of someone else's, forgets what he himself loses in order lovingly to bear in mind someone else's loss, forgets his advantage in order lovingly to think of someone else's. (*WL*, 281)

SELF-HONESTY

Above all learn from Job to become honest with yourself so that you do not deceive yourself with imagined power, with which you experience imagined victory in imagined struggle. (*EUD*, 123)

SELFISHNESS

There is nothing a human being hangs on to so firmly—indeed, with his whole self!—as to his selfishness! (*FSE*, 77)

SELF-KNOWLEDGE

Self-knowledge is a difficult matter; although it is easy to understand the rest of the world, the understanding suddenly changes very substantially when it pertains to oneself. (*EUD*, 275)

Much of what you could try to keep in obscurity you first get to know by letting an omniscient one become aware of it. (*UDVS*, 23)

SELF-LOVE

A person shall love his neighbor as himself, that is, as he ought to love himself. (*WL*, 23)

SELF-SATISFACTION

Were you always satisfied with yourself, so satisfied that you perhaps thanked God that you were not like other people? (*EUD*, 45)

SELF-TRANSPARENCY

In every person there is something that up to a point hinders him from becoming completely transparent to himself, and this can be the case to such a high degree, he can be so inexplicably intertwined in the life-relations that lie beyond him, that he cannot open himself. But the person who can scarcely open himself cannot love, and the person who cannot love is the unhappiest of all. (*EO*, Part II, 160)

SERVING GOD

If you want to show that your life is intended to serve God, then let it serve people, yet continually with the thought of God. (*WL*, 161)

SERVING TWO MASTERS

"No one can serve two masters"—but just look around once in the world of men, but do not forget to include yourself, and you will perhaps not find a single one about whom it is even approximately true that he serves only one master. It seems, therefore, that it might be possible to serve two masters, since everyone is doing it.

And yet the Gospel says: No one can serve two masters. (*JP*, IV, 470)

SICKNESS OF THE SPIRIT

Just as a physician might say that there very likely is not one single living human being who is completely healthy, so anyone who really knows mankind might say that there is not one single living human being who does not despair a little, who does not secretly harbor an unrest, an inner strife, a disharmony, an anxiety about an unknown something or a something he does not even dare to try to know, an anxiety about some possibility in existence or an anxiety about himself, so that, just as the physician speaks of going around with an illness in the body, he walks around with a sickness, carries around a sickness of the spirit that signals its presence at rare intervals in and through an anxiety he cannot explain. (*SUD*, 22)

SILENCE

The very first thing that must be done is: create silence, bring about silence; God's Word cannot be heard, and if in order to be heard in the hullabaloo it must be shouted deafeningly with noisy instruments, then it is not God's Word; create silence! Ah, everything is noisy; and just as a strong drink is said to stir the blood, so everything in our day, even the most insignificant project, even the most empty communication, is designed merely to jolt the senses or to stir up the masses, the crowd, the public, noise! And man, this clever fellow, seems to have become sleepless in order to invent ever new instruments to increase noise, to spread noise and insignificance with the greatest possible haste and on the greatest possible scale. (*FSE*, 47–48)

There is one thing, and if you forgot to introduce this into your house, your home—the most important thing is lacking—it is: silence! Silence! Silence—it is not a specific something, because it does not consist simply in the absence of speaking. No, silence is like the subdued lighting in a pleasant room, like the friendliness in a modest living room; it is not something one talks about, but it is there and exercises its beneficent power. Silence is like the tone, the fundamental tone, which is not given prominence and is called the fundamental tone precisely because it lies at the base. . . . Silence brought into a house—that is eternity's art of making a house a home! (*FSE*, 49–50)

SIN

Sin is not a matter of a person's not having understood what is right but of his being unwilling to understand it, of his not willing what is right. (*SUD*, 95)

Sin grows every moment that one does not take leave of it. (*SUD*, 106)

SLAYING

In the physical and the external sense, I can fall by the hand of another, but in the spiritual sense there is only one person who can slay me, and that is myself. In the spiritual sense, a murder is inconceivable—after all, no assailant can murder an immortal spirit; spiritually, only suicide is possible. (*WL*, 333)

SLOWNESS

The most crucial issues are decided slowly, little by little, not in haste and all at once. (*EUD*, 199)

SLYNESS

The hypocrisy of reason is infinitely sly. That is why it is so hard to catch sight of. (*D*, 91)

SMUGGLING GOD AWAY THROUGH TRUTH

With the most affable and most appreciative philosophical terminology, people have managed to smuggle God away. They are busy obtaining a truer and truer conception of God but seem to forget the first basic principle: that one ought to fear God. (*CUP,* I, 544)

SOLITUDE

On the whole, the longing for solitude is a sign that there still is spirit in a person and is the measure of what spirit there is. (*SUD,* 64)

SOUL ROT

If a person's soul comes to a standstill in the monotony of self-concern and self-preoccupation, then he is bordering on soul rot. (*EUD,* 207)

STANDING STILL

The person who has come to faith (whether he is extraordinarily gifted or plain and simple does not matter) does not come to a standstill in faith. Indeed, he would be indignant if anyone said this to him, just as the lover would resent it if someone said that he came to a standstill in love; for, he would answer, I am by no means standing still. I have my whole life in it. (*FT,* 122–23)

SUCKING GRIEF OUT OF THE PAST

Even if you are conscious of having suffered greatly and the human supposition arises in your soul that it will eventually come to an end and better times will be coming, what good is it for you if you merely stare at the past and suck new grief out of it instead of rejoicing that the hour of liberation will perhaps strike soon. You may become so enervated that you will not be able to hear the sound when it does strike. (*JP*, II, 495)

SUFFERING

It is certainly true that through sufferings a person comes to know a great deal about the world, how deceitful and treacherous it is, and much else like that, but all this knowledge is not the schooling of sufferings. No, just as we speak of a child's having to be weaned when it no longer is allowed to be as one with the mother, so also in the most profound sense a person must be weaned by sufferings, weaned from the world and the things of this world, from loving it and from being embittered by it, in order to learn for eternity. Therefore the school of sufferings is a *dying to* and quiet lessons in *dying to*. (*UDVS*, 257)

SUNDAYS AND MONDAYS

A child can understand it; the simplest person can understand, just as it is stated, that we are capable of nothing at all, that we should give up everything, renounce everything. On Sundays it is understood terribly easily (yes, terribly, because this easiness often enough goes the same way as good intentions) *in abstracto*, and on Mondays it is so very difficult to understand that it is this little and specific thing within the relative and concrete existence in which the individual has his daily life, in which the powerful one is tempted to forget humility and the lowly one to mistake relative modesty toward people of status for humility before God. (*CUP*, I, 467)

T

Terror may be the most agitating of emotions. Consider a couple of examples. You are lying in bed, alone and almost asleep, when you hear quiet steps in the house. Slowly the steps get nearer and nearer. They approach the bedroom door and your heart thumps. Or imagine that you have invested your identity in your job. You have devoted countless faithful hours to it and cannot picture yourself not having it. One day you hear that it might be eliminated. You become alarmed and frightened, fearful that you will lose your whole life.

Kierkegaard recommends that we develop "moral terror." By this he means that we develop an aversion, perhaps even a dread and a fright, to sin, guilt, pain, and danger. He does not mean just any pain and danger, but moral pain and moral danger. The idea is for us to be so alarmed at their prospect that we will turn away from them. Put positively, the idea is for us so to love the good that we will move toward it. The truth that Kierkegaard is putting forward is that where there is no moral terror or love of the good, there will be no turning from the bad or upbuilding in the good.

What this truth shows is that a prominent feature of the life of faith is attraction and aversion. The life of faith does not consist just of having the right beliefs; it also consists of cultivating the right attachments and antipathies. On some occasions these need to be fervent and fiery.

∾

TEMPTATION

Evil always tempts with a winsome form and then throws off the mask and allows its victim to sink into the abyss with the thought that it is too late. (*EUD*, 357)

TERROR AND UPBUILDING

Where there is nothing terrifying whatever and no terror whatever, there is nothing that builds up either, no upbuilding whatever. There is forgiveness of sin—that is upbuilding. The terrifying is that there is sin, and the magnitude of the terror in the inwardness of guilt-consciousness is proportionate to the dimension of the upbuilding. There is healing for all pain, victory in all strife, rescue in all danger—that is upbuilding. The terrifying is that there is pain, strife, danger; and the magnitude of the terrifying and the terror is proportionate to what builds up and to the upbuilding. (*CD*, 96)

THINKERS

Alas, the age of thinkers seems to be past! The quiet patience, the humble and obedient slowness, the noble renunciation of momentary influence, the distance of infinity from the moment, the love devoted to one's God and to one's idea, which are necessary to think one thought—this seems to be disappearing; this is almost at the point of becoming ludicrousness to people. (*WL*, 368)

TIME AND ETERNITY

The earth is beautiful enough as a biding place for the person who expects an eternity, but not sufficiently beautiful to cause someone to forget that one is still only on the way. (*EUD*, 261)

One who esteems the temporal will gradually be rendered incapable of being attentive to the eternal, and one in whose eyes the things of this earth remain estimable will gradually lose the capacity to prize the things of heaven. (*EUD*, 266)

TRAITOR

Oh, there is a lot of talk in the world about treachery and faithlessness, and, God help us, it is unfortunately all too true, but still let us never because of this forget that the most dangerous traitor of all is the one every person has within himself. (*WL*, 23)

TRUTH

It is far from being the case that men regard the relationship to truth, relating themselves to the truth, as the highest good, and it is very far from being the case that they Socratically regard being in error in this manner as the worst misfortune—the sensate in them usually far outweighs their intellectuality. (*SUD*, 42–43)

TWO WILLS

Everyone in despair has two wills, one that he futilely wants to follow entirely, and one that he futilely wants to get rid of entirely. (*UDVS*, 30)

Just as a person, despite all his defiance, does not have the power to tear himself away completely from the good, because it is the stronger, he also does not even have the power to will it completely. (*UDVS*, 33)

U–Z

Kierkegaard had mixed sentiments about human understanding. On the one hand, he wanted his readers to understand the ways in which they run from God. He encouraged self-reflection and comprehension of Christian truths. And he asserted that people comprehend very clearly what Christianity requires of them. So he held reason and understanding in high esteem.

On the other hand, he declared that we use reason and understanding to evade what we know Christianity requires of us. We investigate immortality and death in abstract and general ways instead of asking how they make a difference to our everyday lives. (See "Immortality.") We make our understanding of significant spiritual truths impersonal and objective, thereby undermining earnestness toward living out these truths. (See "Objectivity.") Moreover, simply understanding what Christianity requires is not enough to move us to action.

Understanding must, therefore, be supplemented with willing, Kierkegaard stated. He used a number of phrases that explain what he meant by willing. Willing is an "infinite, personal, impassioned interestedness" (*CUP*, I, 29). It is wanting to be healed. It is an internal act—"if the task is to become subjective, then for the individual subject to think death is not at all some such thing in general but is an act" (*CUP*, I, 169).

Of course, this willing must be directed toward the good if understanding is to be supplemented in the proper way. It cannot be resistance against the good or defiance of the good.

If now we ask how it comes about that we will the good instead of defying it, or vice versa, we come to what may be a mystery. We can investigate how understanding and willing interact, how, that is, our understanding of the good affects our willing, or how our willing influences our understanding, but we still can ask, "Why did the will go one way rather than the other?" We can investigate evasions and look at the simple message of the New Testament, but we still do not know why the will inclines toward the one rather than the other.

It looks as if we will have to leave the mystery as is. Though Kierkegaard has illuminated the subtleties of understanding and willing, it seems impossible to explain how the rock-bottom willing takes place. That, however, may not matter so far as the moral life is concerned, for all that we need to know in order to live well is that the will can go in both ways. If we know this much, we are farther along in our journey to God than if we are oblivious of it.

∾

UNDERSTANDING AND DISPOSITION

Fundamentally all understanding depends upon how one is disposed toward something. If a misfortune happens on a day one is really trusting and full of faith—well, even if it were utterly calamitous—if he is trusting and full of faith, he can explain it in various ways in the context of his joy—that God is letting something happen to him simply because now he has the strength to bear it, that now he is to use the occasion to learn to know himself in surmounting it, etc.—If a person is despondent, broken-hearted, melancholy—the most insignificant matter is enough to make him suspect bad luck, the law of fatality, in what happens.

From this we see that a person's whole view of life actually is a confession of the state of his inner being. (*JP*, IV, 354)

UNDERSTANDING THE NEW TESTAMENT

The matter is quite simple. The New Testament is very easy to understand. But we human beings are really a bunch of scheming swindlers; we pretend to be unable to understand it because we understand very well that the minute we understand we are obliged to act accordingly at once. (*JP*, III, 270)

VANITY AND DEATH

To the vain person, the mirror of life sometimes depicts his dissimilarity with flattering faithfulness, but the mirror of death does not flatter; its faithfulness shows all to be identical; they all look alike when death with its mirror has demonstrated that the dead person is silent. (*TDIO*, 86)

WANTING TO BE HEALED

When a man is sick or indisposed, the first thing he does is to send for the physician, and medication is what he wants;

spiritually it is just the opposite—when a man has sinned, the last thing he wants is the physician and medicine. (*JP*, IV, 119)

WEALTH

Earthly wealth always looks poor in relation to death. (*CD*, 17)

Wealth and abundance come hypocritically in sheep's clothing under the guise of safeguarding against cares and then themselves become the object of care, become *the care*. They safeguard a person against cares just as well as the wolf assigned to look after the sheep safeguards these against—the wolf. (*CD*, 23)

WILLING THE GOOD

To will the good for the sake of reward is double-mindedness; therefore to will one thing is to will the good without regard for reward; in truth to will one thing is to will the good but not to want the reward for it in the world. Quite true, the reward may indeed come without a person's willing it; it can come from God also in the external realm, but if he bears in mind that all rewards in the external realm can become what the world's reward always is, a temptation for him, then he must, in order really to be able to will the good, defend himself against the reward. (*UDVS*, 39)

In the busy life, in all the dealings from morning to night, it is not such a scrupulous matter whether a person completely wills the good—as long as he is enterprising, not to mention a thief, in his job, as long as he saves and accumulates, as long as he has a good reputation and, incidentally, avoids scandal. (*UDVS*, 66)

WITHOUT WORSHIP

Think how impoverished a person would be if he could live through life, proud and self-satisfied, without ever having admired anything. But how horrible if a person could live through his life without ever having wondered over God, without ever, out of wonder over God, having lost himself in worship! (*CD*, 132)

WONDER

There is truly only one eternal object of wonder—that is God —and only one possible hindrance to wonder—and that is a person when he himself wants to be something. (*EUD*, 226)

WORKING AGAINST OURSELVES

Ah, if one looks at people's lives, one often must say in sorrow: They do not themselves know what powers they have; they more or less keep themselves from finding that out, because they are using most of their powers to work against themselves. (*UDVS*, 296)

THE WORLD

The world can be possessed only by its possessing me, and this in turn is the way it possesses the person who has won the world. (*EUD*, 164)

That a Christian would not have the same desires and passions that the world has the world cannot get into its head at all (and then it is not true either). But if he does have them, then the world can even less get it into its head why he, out of fear of someone invisible, is so daft as to want to control these, in the world's view innocent and permissible, desires that it is even "a duty to acquire"; why he wants to control the self-love that the world calls not only innocent but laudable; why he wants to control the anger that the world not only regards as natural but as the mark of a man and a man's honor; why he then wants to make himself doubly unhappy: first by not satisfying the desires and next, for his reward, by being ridiculed by the world. (*WL*, 204)

WORLDLY EXPLOITS

Let worldly exploits become greater and greater, more and more extraordinary, more and more complicated, but do not forget that what a person gains by taking part in them, indeed, by managing the greatest of human enterprises, is not worth picking up on the beaten path compared with being superfluous in the world but sharing with God. (*EUD*, 371)

WORRY

All *worldly* worry has its basis in a person's unwillingness to be contented with being a human being, in his worried craving for distinction by way of comparison. (*UDVS*, 171)

YOUTH

In another sense, youth is but vanity, and longing for it even more vanity, "for charm is deceptive, and beauty is vain" (Proverbs 31:30), and the fickle mind dashes away with fleeting hope, and the dance ends, and the joke is forgotten, and strength vanishes, and youth is past, and its place knows it no more; but youth's thought of the Creator is a rosebud that does not wither, because it does not know the time of the year or of the years, and it is the child's most beautiful ornament, and the bride's most beautiful jewel, and the dying person's best garment. (*EUD*, 250–51)

PERMISSIONS *and* ACKNOWLEDGEMENTS

Søren Kierkegaard. *Christian Discourses* and *The Crisis and a Crisis in the Life of an Actress*. Edited and translated by Howard V. Hong and Edna H. Hong. © 1997 Princeton University Press. Reprinted by permission of Princeton University Press.

Søren Kierkegaard. *Concluding Unscientific Postscript to* Philosophical Fragments, Vol. I. Edited and translated by Howard V. Hong and Edna H. Hong. © 1992 Princeton University Press. Reprinted by permission of Princeton University Press.

Søren Kierkegaard. *The Diary of Søren Kierkegaard*. Edited by Peter P. Rohde. © 1960 Philosophical Library, Inc. Published by Carol Publishing Group, 1990.

Søren Kierkegaard. *Eighteen Upbuilding Discourses*. Edited and translated by Howard V. Hong and Edna H. Hong. © 1990 Princeton University Press. Reprinted by permission of Princeton University Press.

Søren Kierkegaard. *Either/Or,* Part II. Edited and translated by Howard V. Hong and Edna H. Hong. © 1987 Princeton University Press. Reprinted by permission of Princeton University Press.

Søren Kierkegaard. *Fear and Trembling* and *Repetition*. Edited and translated by Howard V. Hong and Edna H. Hong. © 1983 Princeton University Press. Reprinted by permission of Princeton University Press.

Søren Kierkegaard. *Works of Love.* Edited and translated by Howard V. Hong and Edna H. Hong. © 1995 Princeton University Press. Reprinted by permission of Princeton University Press.

* The first of the three discourses in this book, "An Occasional Discourse," is often known as *Purity of Heart Is to Will One Thing,* which has been published separately as a Harper Torchbook, translated by Douglas Steere (1956).